Uninterrupted Thoughts

Alicia S. Azahar

Uninterrupted Thoughts

By Alicia S. Azahar

Cover Designed by Jaden Machado

Published by Jazzy Kitty Publications

Logo Designed by LeRoy Grayson

Editor: Anelda L. Attaway

© 2022 Alicia S. Azahar

ISBN 978-1-954425-50-7

Library of Congress Control Number: 2022909802

DEDICATION

I dedicate this book to everyone who is searching the world trying to find their purpose! Look within yourselves, but most of all, look to God because there is where your purpose lies! Remember, it's never too late to start your journey, just get up and start walking!

ACKNOWLEDGMENTS

First given praises and honor to my Lord and Savior Jesus Christ! I wouldn't be who I am today without the love and guidance from above.

A special thank you to my father, Patrick Johnson, mothers, Shana Johnson and Felicia Stoker (R.I.P.), grandmothers, Frankie Lee Johnson, Katie Lou Stoker (R.I.P) and Mardelle Clayton (R.I.P.), I am who I am because of your love, prayers and teachings.

To the love of my life, my husband, Gilbert Azahar, thank you for being with me every step of the way, loving, supporting and believing in me. I couldn't have done this alone!

To my beautiful children Kai and Katrice, mommy loves you both so much! Thank you for supporting me and enduring this long journey. I pray I make you both proud!

To my sisters and brothers Ashley, Aisha, PJ, Ashanti, and Alijah! You all are the best siblings a woman could ever ask for! I love you all deeply and I'm so grateful for your love and support throughout the years! Last but not least, my extended family, friends and anyone who bought this book, thank you for believing in me and encouraging me on this journey! You are appreciated!

A special thank you to Terrhonda Hillman-Armstrong for pushing me to publish this book. To Michael Guinn for his encouragement and introducing me to Jazzy Kitty Publications.

TABLE OF CONTENTS

TABLE OF CONTENTS

TABLE OF CONTENTS

TABLE OF CONTENTS

INTRODUCTION

This eclectic collection of poetry takes you on an uninterrupted journey of love, laughter, pain, loss and discovery! Written from the creative mindset of a spoken word artist, you will certainly leave feeling inspired, loved and with a better understanding of who Alicia Azahar is! This poet speaks from her heart to yours with her unique style of writing. You will laugh, cry, get upset, and fall in love by the influence of her powerful word flow, but you won't be the same after you finish this book. Come take a ride on these uninterrupted thoughts of poetry train and see the world through her eyes!

A WOMAN

I use to wonder when my body was going to start developing into
a woman,

I know that sounds confusing, but you see, I was told before that
if you have those "childbearing hips,"

The kind that makes a man want to grip and discover your secret
between them,

Then you're a woman,

Because there ain't no way that a woman has a flat chest, or
anything less than C cup breast, right?,

A woman doesn't just sound like a woman, but she looks and
talks like a woman,

Even when she walks by you smell the scent of a woman,

It's hard to describe a woman because there are so many
components,

How she can just walk into a room and downright own it,

From the way her breast hang naturally like teardrops,

To the way, her hips sway will make any man stop,

Women rule the world just by a look,

With her voice soft but yet powerful, have all the men shook,

A woman is one of the most powerful weapons in this world,

We were nuclear weapons ever since little girls,

They call us mythical creatures because there ain't nothing like us,

Gotta have a dictionary to figure out which word to describe us,

In a room full of men, we are the topic of their discussion,

Walk into a club and got all of 'em tusslin',

Because women were, am, is and are,

Against the midnight sky, we are the stars,

Illuminating,

Fascinating,

Elevating,

Captivating,

Got 'em waiting,

For us to come all the way down to their level,

They dig us so hard, we gotta throw 'em a shovel,

A woman is what I am and will always be,

I came from a woman and one came from me,

We are life creating, others imitating, but there's no debating,

That a woman is one of the most amazing creatures that God has

ever made,

A sight so beautiful that your eyes have ever laid,

A woman,

Your mother,

Your daughter,

Your aunt,

Your sister,

Your grandma,

Your cousin,

So don't you dare diss her,

Because a woman is someone you came from you see,

And a woman is someone that a man could never be!

ABC'S OF LIFE

Always give your best no matter what you choose to do,

Be a leader and not a follower, remember someone's watching you,

Continue to strive for excellence each and every day,

Don't allow negativity to come lead you astray,

Encourage one another and speak life into your peers,

Face your problems head-on and don't give in to your fears,

Goals are very important, make sure you set them for yourself,

Help is there when you need to get it from someone else,

Inspiration is all around, you don't have to look very far,

Join a group of successful people who will help set the bar,

Keep a smile on your face and always try to be kind,

Live your life with a purpose and always keep it on your mind,

Manage time like it's money because you don't have time to waste,

Never give up on yourself, no matter what others say,

Optimism will get you far, so always look at the brighter side,

Pride comes before the fall, so remain humble inside,

Quitters never win and winners never quit,

Remember, life is a marathon, so there is no need to sprint,

Stay away from bad places and watch who you're surrounded by,

Take a moment to be grateful for everything in your life,

Understand that life is short, pursue your dreams while you can,

Voice your opinion when necessary, but be sure of your demands,

Words are powerful, so please be careful of what you choose to say,

Xtend a helping hand to others and guide them on their way,

You are what you eat, be mindful of what you consume,

Zero in on the things that you want to improve!

ALL I CAN SAY

What can I say that hasn't already been said mama?

From the day that my heart was ripped out of my chest from your death,

That moment you took your last breath,

You didn't even have a chance to say goodbye,

And for that, I use to be angry at God, wondering why,

But He knew you had to go in the manner that you did,

Although my sister and I were just kids,

It hurt like getting stung by a honeybee, wait, no a wasp,

Because when a honeybee stings you, their lives are lost,

But a wasp can keep stinging and stinging and stinging you,

And come back again like it wasn't even through,

And that's exactly what it felt like losing you that day,

A moment in time snatched away,

Some sinister video being replayed,

Making me watch it,

Holding me hostage,

Demanding a ransom for my sorrow,

Me praying to God for tomorrow,

Begging time to let me borrow,

Just a few minutes so that I can hold you one last time,

A second for you to say what was on your mind,

An hour of the day before you died to rewind,

What would you have said to my sister and I?

That you didn't know you were going to die?

That if you did know, then you would've tried?

To stop death from sneaking in through the back door,

You would've stopped it in its tracks and slammed it on the floor,

And told it that you were staying another day to hold us once more?

Knowing you mama, you would've fought like crazy,

Just to spend another hour with your babies,

And sometimes I feel like death robbed us from that moment,

How much of a coward it is to own it,

Would death be scared if I came for it too?

Would it run and hide like some people try to do?

Only to be snatched up like a hawk does its prey,

Laughing because it knows it can't get away,

Your number was pulled and that day was your day,

Oh, how I wish that you could've stayed,

But, I miss you mama, is all I can say!

AN APPLE A DAY

I was told an apple a day keeps the doctor away, but nothing can keep my love from you,

You're the Folgers to my cup because "the best part of waking up" is being right next to you,

If I were to describe our love, it would be like Ajax, "stronger than dirt" mixed with Coca Cola "it's the real thing!"

L'Oréal couldn't have said it better "because you're worth it!" is all my heart wants to sing,

I knew you were the one just like Apple you "think different" than all of the others,

Your love for me has "no bounty" and when I'm down, you're "the quicker picker-upper!,"

No matter what obstacles we face Avis says, "we try harder" with all of our might,

And if the spark in our relationship starts to dim,

General Electric reminds us, "we bring good things to life!"

We got that American Express type of love because "we don't leave home without it!"

And if I ever left a stain of doubt on your heart, then let me come over and "shout it!,"

You're the greatest of all lovers, and no one else can stand the test,

And just like Hallmark does for others, for me, "you care enough to send the very best!

ART

Art is the existence of our imagination formed by creative skill,

Art is unique and beautiful, art is something real,

Art is the freedom to express our feelings in many different forms,

Art is song and dance, art is writing poems,

Art is a chair that we sit down on to enjoy our favorite meal,

Art is paintings on a wall, art is houses that we build,

Art is love letters that we write to our loved ones far away,

Art expresses how we feel, art is used in what we say

Art is millions of tiny stars surrounded by the midnight sky,

Art is sculptures made of stone, art is baking an apple pie,

Art is spots on a cheetah's body and a peacock's colorful feathers

Art is the color of a tree's leaves changed by the force of weather

Art is the different shades of color of all of our beautiful skin,

Art is the anatomy of our body and the organs held within,

Art is found throughout the world and it allows us to be free,

Art is the very essence of you and me!

AUTUMN

Leaves slip away from the barren limbs that once held them, echoing a crisp thud as they fall on the ground,

The tree weeps as the cruel air strips away its beauty, transforming the light, vibrant splendor to a gravely, dull shade,

Beautiful shades of amber, orange, and gold have now browned in a pile at its feet,

Insects eat away at the leftovers hidden in the carcass of hollow stumps as wildings gather bits of food to ration during the shortage,

Birds begin their journey south, leaving behind empty nests and cracked eggshells,

Streams that once quenched the thirst of its inhabitants silently flow in isolation,

The existence of nature now is nothing more than a silhouette!

BANK ACCOUNT

If I had a dollar for every time, you said, "I'm sorry," I would be a millionaire by now,

Too bad I couldn't deposit your blank apologies because they would be insufficient,

Every one of your "I'm sorry's" over-drafted my hopes that one day you would change,

Causing excessive feelings of regret and resentment,

Me knowing that I couldn't get my time waived that was wasted on you all of these years,

I carefully reviewed the accounts when you told me that I was overreacting or it was "all in my head,"

But now, I found out that you were too busy making deposits into other accounts,

Slowing withdrawing my self-worth over time, only to leave me with a negative balance,

Forcing me to borrow from others because I had nothing

left to give,

How could you be so greedy and deplete everything out of me you claimed made me so special?

If I had a dollar for every time you told me I was beautiful, I would be a millionaire by now,

But yet, I'm broke from your excessive use of my love,

You took my kindness for weakness, and now I have to report you for fraud,

I should've put a stop payment on all of those fake "I love you's" and "I can change's,"

But I believed you when you told me that you were real,

You've bankrupt my heart and now I'm placing all of this bad credit on you,

But I promise it won't take me seven years to get over you,

I'm carefully reviewing these negative inquiries I've accrued over the years and I'm disputing them,

For every time I felt afraid, alone, useless, or broken,

I'm removing them out of my life one by one,

Giving myself credit for now being brave enough to walk away and realizing that I'm good enough,

You no longer have access to my heart, I've removed you from all of my accounts of what I thought we could be,

And now I'm cashing in on my true happiness!

BLACK

When most people think of the color black, they imagine dirty things,

Like oily clothes, blacktop roads, or the darkness that a storm brings,

But I'm here to inform you about the beauty of black, and all of the powers that it possesses, that other colors lack,

Black is not dirty, neither is it unclean, it's what most things are made of, but other colors on top are seen,

It is the color of the night, that illuminates the moon and stars, and the color of roads that are made out of tar,

Black is the absence of color when people close their eyes to sleep, and the darkness of an ocean that is very, very deep,

It is the color of oil, that is used for many things, and the color of musical notes in a song that you sing,

Black is the pen's ink that you use to write, it's what draws other colors to the intensity of light,

It is the color of the words in a book that you read, and the opposite of light in which you need,

Black is freshly brewed coffee in a mug that you drink, and that space between your thoughts whenever you think,

It is the color of the rainbow that are stirred to make one, and your shadow on the ground reflected by the sun,

Black is the color of a bat, black is the color of your shoes,

It is the darkness when you mourn, and the color of a bruise,

Black symbolizes power, black is the color of a zebra's stripes,

It's the color of a panther and smoke from a pipe,

Black is what you see when you write a letter, black is the passion that you feel and the love that makes it better,

It is the color of mystery, it is the color of a pot,

Black is the envy of all colors because it's powers they have not,

It is the emotions you feel when sad or upset,

Black is the confidence you have during that moment you won't forget,

Black is special and used for many things, it is the power that we possess to overcome anything,

It's one of the most beautiful color in this world can't you see, black is honor and love,

Black is me!

BLACK HISTORY

When I think of Black History, what comes to mind is far beyond stories of captivity and slaves,

That all is a part of our history, but let's shine light on those who've helped pave the way,

You see, Black History is more than just stories of our ancestors' trials and perseverance,

They weren't just a group of slaves or servants, it was way more to their appearance,

There are countless people in our history who've made contributions over the years,

A timeline filled with black excellence that has gotten us all here,

There were many inventors, doctors, nurses, musicians and singers,

Poets, authors, painters, bricklayers and Civil rights leaders,

We had boxers, chefs, entrepreneurs, lawyers and educators,

Olympians, pilots, visionaries, judges and legislators,

Some were seamstresses, designers, actors, activists and technicians,

Producers, choreographers, secretaries, generals and lieutenants,

We had scientists, captains, farmers, bookkeepers and flight attendants,

Counselors, preachers, policemen, marines and administrative assistants,

Some were barbers, hairdressers, makeup artists, postal carriers and firemen,

Janitors, stonemasons, butlers, waiters and also cable men,

I can't forget to mention about President and Vice President,

There are hundreds of other positions and roles that are also relevant,

That shines light on our black history that has gotten us all here today,

So, when we say, "Black History," we mean the ones who have helped make a way,

For Black women and men to be anything we could ever imagine to be,

They took their dreams of freedom and a better life and turned it into reality,

Black History is more than just a month and far more beyond a trend,

So, from now on when you think of "Black History," add excellence on the end!

BLANK PAGES

Blank pages mean full minds,

Minds that long to tell stories,

Stories of love, sadness, disappointments and triumphs,

Blank pages mean untold secrets,

Secrets that are hidden behind walls of distrust and agony,

Agony from broken promises that were once welcomed with gentle kisses,

Kisses that were laced with poisoned lips and deceitful tongues,

Blank pages mean guarded hearts,

Hearts that are held captive by fear of being broken,

Now lie shattered on the cold, hard ground,

Blank pages mean silenced voices,

Voices that are screaming to be heard,

Heard by listening ears on familiar faces,

Faces that once hid from ugly truths and beautiful lies,

Blank pages mean nothing unless you are willing to write your story,

Stories that have never been told or heard of!

BRUISES

Makeup hides black eyes,

Lipstick covers up busted lips,

Tissue cleans up bloody noses,

From balled up angry fist,

Sweatshirts hide an ugly bruise,

Casts go around broken arms,

Lies cover up the naked truth,

But jealous hearts can cause harm,

Bottles crash against dirty walls,

Children cry as mama screams,

Dishes fall off countertops,

As police pull up at the scene,

Bullets fly out of smoking guns,

White clothes stained with the color red,

Mama's body is laying still,

As police tell me that she's dead!

BULLY

It's that time of day again and the bell just rang for lunch,

I'm hiding in the bathroom, hoping today I don't get punched,

My body's sore from yesterday, my left eye's colored black,

My lip is still real swollen from when I was attacked,

I never saw it coming, I was just walking down the hall,

I heard him shout my name before my head hit the wall,

I don't know all the details everything just faded black,

One minute I was up and walking,

the next thing I'm on my back,

I woke up in the nurse's office with an ice pack on my head,

"Do you know what happened?" is the first thing that she said,

I shook my head real slowly, and muttered, "No, I don't recall",

I was scared to tell the truth and so I began to ball,

This was not my first encounter with a bully from a school,

And it always tends to happen to the ones who seem uncool,

I try to go unnoticed to take the target off my back,

But somehow, I gain attraction because strength I seem to lack,

I try to hide my fear and always stand up for myself,

But when I get knocked down, no one seems to want to help,

How can we make them stop?

If no one's willing to take a stand,

"Just say no to bullying," should be all of our demand,

But these crimes will carry on

unless we reach out to the youth,

Parents need to be more involved

because they're blinded from the truth,

So, let's do what we can do now and get a move on it fast,

Because you never know one day, it could be your child's last!

CHICKEN SKIN

I don't know what it is about you, I just can't seem to get enough,

You're tempting to my eyes, but even better to the touch,

Your salty, crunchy texture really does something to me,

One bite just won't do the trick, I need another sixty three,

A delightful crunch is what I hear when I sink my teeth in,

You're the best part of my meal, crispy brown chicken skin,

I could eat you in a salad, I could eat you by yourself,

I ignore when people tell me, you aren't good for my health,

We have a special kind of bond people just don't have a clue,

If they knew how good you taste they would be talking about you too,

Some people disrespect your goodness by buying skinless for their meat,

But your skin's what makes you special, no skinless meat could ever be,

I'll always celebrate your goodness even if I don't fit in,

I love you now and forever my crispy, brown chicken skin!

DIABETES AWARENESS

What is diabetes and can it happen to you?

The two most common kinds are Type 1 and Type 2,

It doesn't always come from poor eating habits or being overweight,

Some people are born with this disease no matter what they put on their plate,

Type 1 is mainly caused when your pancreas produces little to no insulin,

It's also known as juvenile diabetes typically appearing in adolescence,

Many people aren't aware of all of the signs at first,

Blurred vision, increased hunger, frequent urination and thirst,

Type 1 is not curable, but different treatments can help,

Exercising, diets, hormones, or insulin injections on self,

Type 2 symptoms may be reversible, but it depends on what you do,

Although a cure is not an option, diet and exercise may help you,

Some people monitor their glucose levels with a meter every day,

Using a needle to prick their fingers while sugar levels are displayed,

Insulin is normally taken by injection or in a pill,

Most of the time people take it after they've eaten a meal,

Millions of people have diabetes, doctors are diagnosing every day,

This disease is all around no matter where you choose to stay,

Diabetes can come as a surprise and often give people a scare,

So, make sure to educate yourselves and always stay aware!

DON'T FORGET YOUR MANNERS

We shouldn't need reminders on how to be polite and sweet,

For some it comes real natural when in public or whom we meet,

Saying "hello" and "good morning" are pleasant ways to start your day,

And you can even say it back if you don't know what to say,

"Good afternoon" is often used between the hours of 12 and 6,

And we normally say, "good evening" while fixing dinner for the kids,

"Please" and "thank you" are exchanged for our requests here and there,

Don't forget to say, "you're welcome" to show how much you really care,

When in a hurry mind your manners, say, "excuse me" with a smile,

If you see something you want saying, "may I" is still in style,

You should never feel uneasy being pleasant to your neighbor,

And when your conversation is over politely say, "talk to you later,"

Using manners throughout the day can put a smile on someone's face,

You never know when your words may brighten up a cloudy day,

"Thank you" for your time and listening to my list of standards,

Please remember to be kind and don't forget to use your manners!

EXCEL

What does excellence look like? I'm staring at it here today,

Being excellent isn't just an act,

but can be used in what we say,

It's displayed in our ability to strive for merit in all we do,

It's shown by pursuing our dreams until they do come true,

It's not just about good grades and being the star of the team,

Excellence is guided by our vision to make our realities seen,

It's well beyond what's measured on our standard scale of feat,

Excellence is defined by our persistence

even when we face defeat,

It's shown by how we live our lives

and in the choices that we make,

Excellence is shown in our efforts

and in the risks that we take,

So, stay focused on your task

and in everything you will do well,

Not just today, not just tomorrow,

but every day you will excel!

FAREWELL 2020

Dear 2020,

We heard that you were leaving soon so we thought we'd give you a proper farewell,

This past year has been a rollercoaster for us, but for some it was pure hell,

You just couldn't leave quietly, could you? You had to go and cause a big scene,

As if Covid wasn't enough for us, you went and pulled other schemes,

Political wars, violence, and racial tension to name a few,

Unemployment and depression, some people lost their homes too,

But what do you even care? You're about to leave in several weeks,

Do us a favor, never come back and whatever you take it's yours to keep,

We never thought we'd be so excited to see this year pass on by,

But believe us when we tell you, when you leave we will not cry,

We will not shed a single tear for you because we did enough of that already,

On a level of one to ten you're one thousand times more petty,

You just sat back, watched and laughed as all hell broke loose,

You'd think twice before laughing if you had to walk a day in our shoes,

But it's okay, we don't hate you; you gave us a reason to keep on living,

When we look back over this year, we had a whole lot of "thanks given,"

You see, you made us a lot stronger than we ever thought that we could be,

Even though we were quarantined it made us spend more time with our families,

You helped us save a lot of money by keeping our children out of school,

And did we mention we saved on gas with all of these mandatory "shut down" rules,

The holidays weren't the same, but it made us love our families more,

It made us appreciate the times we took for granted once before,

Although you stole a lot from us, you gave us back more than you know,

We were the real stars of 2020, you just put on the show,

You thought that you could break us, but we're more grateful in the end,

So, farewell 2020 we hope we never see you again!

FATHER

There are many ways to say, "father" such as: daddy, pops, dad, papa and my old man,

I'm just grateful I can call you what not everyone else can,

You've been my father for many years, one day of recognition just isn't enough,

Only a true father can do the things that you've done that's why I love you so much,

A father just isn't a provider it goes way deeper than a title,

You taught me many lessons throughout my life not just about survival,

I know how to respect others and stand up for what I believe in,

I know how to set goals and do what it takes to achieve them,

You taught me how to save money and pay bills whenever they're due,

You showed me how to exercise my faith and to seek the things that are true,

You showed me how to serve others and to give back to the community,

You taught me the importance of family and that love is the unity,

You showed me how to raise a family and to discipline my children out of love,

You taught me how to pray and to rely on guidance from above,

You've shown me many examples of what it takes to be a parent,

Even when things got tough you didn't let that be a deterrent,

You showed me how to carry myself and to live my life with purpose,

You showed me that you being a father was one of your greatest services,

Being a father wasn't easy, but you have evolved over the years,

You remained present in my life and never chose to disappear,

I can only repay a fraction for everything you've done for me,

But because of your guidance I'm going to do my best to be everything I was taught to be!

FORGIVE

I must learn to forgive, not for you but for me,

I must learn to forgive, to erase the pain inside of me,

I must learn to forgive, so I can move on,

I must learn to forgive, so hurt get gone,

I must learn to forgive, so I can have peace,

I must learn to forgive, so I can live free,

I must learn to forgive, that's all I can do,

Because I have to forgive, to get over you!

FREEDOM

Skin soaked in honey kissed by the sun,

Hair curlier than wool coming undone,

Lips full like two pillows stuffed with feathers,

Shoulders broad as the horizon in the Sahara desert,

Eyes brighter than the stars twinkling in the night,

Teeth standing like pillars all pearly and white,

Hands strong and steady like beams in a roof,

Bones thicker than grits stirred with a spoon,

Voices booming like thunder full of ancestors' songs,

Weary nights on the trail hoping to see dawn,

Hungry stomachs being filled with bits of cornbread,

Tired feet carefully walking on the path they are led,

Hopeful souls quickly follow the stars as they see them,

Scarred backs carrying children to a life of freedom!

GOOD MAN

You say you want a good man who knows how to listen,

You say he must go to church, but you ain't even a Christian,

You make all of these demands about how a man is suppose to be,

But yet, you don't know how to cook, clean, or shop for groceries,

You say he must have a job, his own car, and a home,

But yet you still live with your parents and don't have it for your own,

You say he must treat you good, and come home every night,

But yet, you stay in clubs all hours always starting fights,

You say he must be faithful and never look at other women,

But yet, you post dirty pictures on social media to fit in,

You say he must be loyal and always treat you like a queen,

But yet, you act like a jester, now that's not fit for a king,

You say he must know how to mow, take out trash and change a flat,

But yet, you can't take care of home because you're always on your back,

You say he must be a leader and take charge in every way,

But yet, you don't know how to listen, be his rib, or even pray,

You say that he must treat you with love and respect at all times,

But yet, you don't even respect yourself, now that should be a crime,

You say he must be handsome, dress nice and smell real good,

But yet, you don't take care of your body the way you really should,

You say he must pay your bills, buy you expensive clothes and shoes,

But yet, you call him superficial, but have materialistic point of views,

You say you want a good man to marry you and raise a family,

But yet, you don't know the first thing about what a "good woman" is suppose to be.

GOODBYE

How do I say, "goodbye" to a place that was once my home?

To the relationships that were built with the people I got to know,

How do I say, "goodbye" to my friends I'm about to leave?

To the warm "hellos" and "good mornings" I once did receive,

How do I say, "goodbye" to the ones I grew fond of?

To the jokes and all of the laughter, I once use to love,

How do I say, "goodbye" at a time such as this?

To the conversations that we've had that I'm now going to miss,

How do I say, "goodbye" to over six years of my life?

To the dedication, hard work and all of the sacrifice,

How do I say, "goodbye" without causing my voice waver?

I guess for now I'll have to leave by just saying, "see you later"

GOSSIP

It spreads like a wildfire or an airborne disease,

Tickling the ears of anyone it please,

Seducing the minds of all who will hear,

Rumors and stories from afar and near,

No facts, just opinions, of what they don't know,

People sharing these tales as they come and go,

Saturating stories with judgment and mess,

Comparing their lives as if they know best,

These rumors leave stains on the victim's reputation,

As people engage in pointless conversations,

But be mindful of the things you choose to do,

Because gossip can also happen to you!

GUILT

I was angry, I needed someone to take the fall for my insecurities,

Unable to hide behind the naked truth that it wasn't you who made me feel this way, but I,

I needed a scapegoat for this emotional cycle that has been tormenting me for years,

"Is he cheating on me?"

"Is he attracted to her?"

All of these questions stemming from my poor decisions and bad relationships,

I had to put the blame on you in order for me not to feel the poison that has been slowly killing me,

Every time I looked in the mirror, I saw each woman,

Her eyes, her face, her nose, her lips, smiling back at me, laughing at my brokenness,

Mocking the fact that he chose her over me,

I hated myself for being too weak to leave when I had the chance,

I punished myself each day I stayed and welcomed those infidelities and betrayals,

But now I have you, an innocent bystander,

Struck by my emotional bullets of distrust, paranoia, and bitterness,

I watch through my rearview mirror of pain as you lay there slowly bleeding out,

Calling for help, but no one will come to save you,

I drive off, adrenaline coursing through my veins,

Unable to shake the fact that I put a hit out on your heart,

Every shot fired screaming at you for what he did,

I'm scared because those bullets of bad decisions, regret, and hurt were not meant for you, but for him,

You were in the wrong place at the right time, but unfortunately time wasn't on your side,

I'm on the run now, evading the imprisonment that is waiting for me,

Afraid to pull over and turn myself in for this horrible crime against you,

There were no witnesses to identify what I had done to you,

Only you would be able to point me out in the lineup of broken women,

Women who've stayed one second, one minute, one hour and one day too long in bad relationships,

Sadly, you were the one put on trial and found guilty for other men's crimes,

Sentenced to a lifetime of fixing mistakes, reassuring insecurities, and building back walls of trust,

But, it's too late for you, you've been thrown into an empty cell,

With nothing but bad memories, unanswered questions, and

regret from every broken heart you couldn't repair,

And now your innocence has become my guilt!

HERE AT HUMANA

We're not your average pharmacy, we stand out above the rest,

We put the HUMAN in Humana, to make your experience the best,

We cater to all of our members, young and old, near and far,

We'll send your prescriptions through the mail, just in case you don't have a car,

Don't worry about your maintenance drugs, we'll ship you three months in advance,

We'll set you up for refill reminders, whenever you get the chance,

Just in case you're in a hurry, put our self-service apps to use,

We'll tell you just where to find them, so that you can pick and choose,

If your prescriptions have copayments, we offer ways to pay your bill,

Check by phone, money orders, or credit cards to set the deal,

Several hundreds of agents available, for your convenience day and night,

Solving problems for our members, to make their heavy burdens light,

You are more than just a number, we treat each member like our own,

Because here at Humana Pharmacy, we'll make you feel right at home!

HIDDEN

Some things are better hidden behind the veil,

I can't depict fantasy from reality, it's too hard to tell,

You want me to uncover your heaven, but the reality is hell,

Hypnotized from this darkness you've got me under your spell,

I'm breathless, shameless, my mind is going insane,

But loving you isn't easy and hating you is too much pain,

So, let's unwind for a minute and stop the time from pressing on,

I can't stand it when I'm with you, but I hate it when you're gone.

HIDE AND GO SEEK

"Hide and Go Seek" use to be my favorite game to play as a child,

The thrill of hiding in a place where I never thought a person could ever find me,

Closets, underneath beds, bathroom cabinets, behind doors or couches,

I remember that intense feeling of panic as someone came near my hiding spot,

I'd hold my breath while listening to their sneaky footsteps tiptoeing around hoping to find me,

My heartbeat pounding in my ears as I suddenly became lightheaded from the lack of oxygen,

And then suddenly I'd hear the soft thud of footsteps echoing as they moved further away,

It seemed like an eternity, hiding, waiting, hoping and praying to not get caught,

Once I heard the exasperation and groaning of defeat from my intended captor,

I'd jump out of my hiding place and triumphantly say, "I win!",

Soon that game was no longer fun for me, it transformed into this intense act of survival mode,

I can still smell the sour, pungent odor of beer and cigarettes on his breath,

The heaviness of the air surrounding and suffocating me while he clumsily unzipped his work pants and demanded me to walk over to him,

His eyes piercing through mine, burning a hole in my head as he grabbed my hand and made me touch it,

That was the first time I think I ever felt intensely sick to my stomach to the point where I actually vomited a little in my mouth,

I can still smell his musty, sweaty skin soaked in 12 hours' worth of a day's work,

My hands trembling with fear as he coached me on what to do and how to do it,

His head rolling back, moaning and panting at the mere pleasure he was receiving from me,

His daughter,

A child,

That was the first of many times he made me do it,

No amount of bleach could blot out the stain of guilt and shame that he left on my hands,

I hated him, despised him, but somehow still pitied his broken, wounded spirit,

For some reason, I felt conflicted every time I was forced to do that despicable thing for him,

When he was sober, he was almost sweet, caring and human,

He'd randomly buy me ice cream whenever I went with him to run errands in town,

The car rides would be peaceful as soft melodies played over the radio,

I would roll the window down and allow the cool breeze to brush against my hot, sticky face,

Occasionally he would touch my thigh with his hand while the other one gripped the steering wheel,

I'd freeze for a moment and shamefully look over at him,

Afraid of what was about to happen, but then he'd give me this warm, reassuring smile,

My shoulders would drop and my heart would sink back into my chest as he would sing the lyrics to whatever song was playing in the background,

Those car rides, those few, beautiful sober moments I had with him almost made me forget about the monster he truly was,

About how he used me to fulfill his dirty, evil, lustful desires,

Those constant nightmares I had of his abuse replayed over and over and over,

Images of it coming towards me and filling my hands up with this sticky substance,

Me crying and disgusted at the sight, running to the bathroom to grab a bottle of bleach and baptize my hands in it,

Washing them for what seemed like an eternity, but no matter how hot the water was,

The stinging pain of my skin boiling underneath the running faucet,

That sin never washed away,

I've carried that guilt, resentment and pain for many years now,

A weight so heavy that these scarred hands can no longer hold on to,

That little girl hides inside this shell called woman,

Seeking healing and forgiveness, but do I have the courage to go find her?

I MISS SUNDAYS

I miss Sundays after church when my family would get together,

Fried chicken, cornbread and cabbage with bell peppers,

I couldn't wait until Sunday to see all of my cousins,

The smell of granny's peach cobbler baking in the oven,

Granny's house was the spot for us all to hang out,

Dominoes slapping on the table as us kids ran about,

Our aunts in the kitchen making us a plate,

Sneaky hands grabbing bits of granny's pound cake,

Scarfing down food so we can go outside and play,

Volleyball was the highlight of our entire day,

Joking with one another, laughter all around,

Basketballs bouncing all over the ground,

Whatever happened to Sunday's at granny's house?,

Nowadays it seems like no one wants to come out,

Except at funerals, weddings or when someone gets ill,

I miss sitting as a family and praying before meals,

We've all gone our separate ways, no sense of community,

Granny's house is what kept us all in unity,

We need to get back together like we use to before,

Greetings passed all around as we walked through the door,

Granny's house was the heart of all of our get togethers,

Fish fry's, barbecues, nothing seemed better,

Elders sharing stories from back in the day,

Family secrets being told while sending nosy kids away,

Sundays at granny's house was like a reunion each week,

Passing out hugs and giving kisses on the cheek,

I miss Sundays after church when my family would get together,

A lifetime of memories that I'll always treasure!

I NEED YOU

Lord, I need a breakthrough, I feel like my back is against the wall,

You're the only one I can run to or even trust to call,

My friends don't understand me and my family's too busy to even help,

But I know that I'm the weakest when I try to do things by myself,

My burden is too much to carry, but I know that you are very strong,

I can't seem to do things right, but I know you'll correct my every wrong,

I get angry when I fail and things don't seem to go my way,

I know you told me to have patience, but sometimes I struggle to obey,

My faith is a like shaky and my confidence is on the ground,

But I know that if I just follow you, you'll turn everything right around,

I couldn't ask for a better friend to pull me through my darkest times,

Sometimes I want to run away, but in you, hope, is what I'll find,

I know this pain is but for a moment, and very soon it will pass on,

Even though the night surrounds me, you'll bring me to the early dawn,

I can feel your presence around me, still at times I wished that I could see you,

But I know where my help comes from, Lord, and right now I really need you!

I SHOULD'VE WAITED

"It's not that big of a deal, you need to get with the times,"

His words constantly float in the back of my mind,

I mean everyone's doing it, what could it hurt?

But will I still be happy and have self-worth?

If I give in this time then he'll leave me alone,

And plus, tonight my parents won't be home,

I'll invite him over for an hour or two,

We'll Netflix and chill until we decide what to do,

It'll be our secret, I know he won't tell,

I'll give him what he wants so that he won't bail,

We've dated three months, but it feels like forever,

And he promised me a ring and a lifetime together,

He tells me he loves me, and that he'll never leave,

And when someone says, "I love you," you have to believe,

He's always concerned about my well-being,

And he asks if he's the only one I'm seeing,

I always say, "yes" and ask him, "why?"

He tells me he wants to be my only guy,

He brings me gifts and sends sweet texts,

And calls me at night before I go to bed,

He's done so much to prove he's the one,

So, I owe him this "gift" for all that he's done,

And tonight, will mark the proof of our love,

Nothing will change it will stay like it was,

He finally comes over and I give in to him,

But it was nothing at all how I imagined,

He leaves to go home without a kiss "goodbye",

And when I text the next day he doesn't reply,

I arrive at school and walk the halls alone,

But the look on kids' faces tells me something is wrong,

I rush over to my locker and find a note inside,

With my name on a list and a check mark beside,

I'm fighting back my tears as he's coming down the hall,

I call out his name but he turns toward the wall,

I suddenly realize it was a snake that I dated,

And I gave away my "gift" when I should've waited.

INSECURE

I see you, but I'm unsure if you're aware,

That same look you're giving her, was once the same look you gave me,

Your eyes close in on her beauty, captivated by her essence,

You gaze at her for one second too long and are suddenly caught off guard by my glare,

You pause for a moment, trying to conjure up a clever excuse as to why your eyes were fixated in that direction,

Unsure of your approach, you swiftly turn your head calculating any vantage point you can find,

Hesitating for a brief moment, you pause to gather your thoughts,

Your tongue is heavy, words stuck to the roof of your mouth like sap on a tree,

You take a deep breath allowing the air to cool your nostrils,

But before your premeditated words can spew out over your lying lips,

They are cut off instantly by mine,

"She's beautiful isn't she?"

Caution warns you to dismiss my statement,

A huge lump forms at the back of your throat, but you're reluctant to swallow it,

You want to agree with me, but past arguments urge you to tread lightly,

"She's okay, not better looking than you!"

I laugh, but not in an amusing way,

I'm disgusted by your dishonesty embodied by cowardice,

You never could be honest with me, as much as you wanted to, you just couldn't,

My eyes search yours with disappointment, but then suddenly I look away,

Your hand reaches for mine, but I angrily snatch it back; hurt, broken, jealous,

Regret sadly escapes your lips gently brushing my ears,

I revert back to those words you've declared to me over the years in my head, but why can't I believe them right now?,

This one critical moment when I need to believe them the most, fall on deaf ears,

Uncertainty showering down on me, drowning my assurance,

And in this moment I realize I'm insecure.

JUDGE

The look in your eyes tells me all I need to know,

Words left unsaid, but in your face they show,

You judge me in a way that pierces to my core,

All the uncertainties you've had from times before,

I'm guilty by your frowns, and also by your eyes,

Convicted by "hellos", sentenced by your "goodbyes,"

I never knew judgement could be cast from a look,

One of disapproval that I often mistook,

I'm judged by your silence from the things that I share,

And the cold disposition you give when you stare,

I'm judged by your sighs, and the shake of you head,

And the opinions you give, with words unsaid,

You never will tell me what you truly think of me,

But I can tell by your face that you judge me.

LET GO AND LET GOD

When situations get too tough and you don't know where to go,

The answer to your every problem is closer than you'll ever know,

Close your eyes, bow your head and call on God's holy name,

He'll meet you right where you're at and still love you all the same,

No matter what you seem to go through He knows just what to do,

He'll fix your problems by himself and restore your broken spirit too,

Go ahead and praise him now although it may seem kind of odd,

Just remember He has your back so let go and let God!

LET HIM GO

"Let him go," this was often said to me,

A woman who was broken with insecurities,

I tried to hold on to pain, only to realize I had nothing to gain,

If I could just make him see that the only woman he needed was me,

But how could I chase after a man that was nothing, but a boy, without a plan?,

No dreams, no drive, no hope or aspirations,

Just greed, just lies, good sex and manipulations,

I stood there empty because I allowed him to take,

The very things that made me, but in his hands would break,

My joy, my peace, my beauty and grace,

My trust, my confidence, he spit back in my face,

But through his web of lies and deceit,

I found out the blame was partially on me,

You see, I allowed myself to stay in this condition,

Hoping that time would buy me another position,

A ring, a title, maybe one day his wife,

But the lies I kept telling myself drove that knife,

Deeper into my heart until I started to bleed out,

The faith I once had in us now turned to doubt,

Hope wasn't enough to soak up what wasn't meant to be,

The fantasy I was lost in now turned reality,

Lies I once told myself, pain I didn't want to show,

All because I was holding onto someone I was suppose to let go.

LIFE

Oh life, how sometimes cruel you can be,

The wonder of so many mysteries,

You invite us in at the beginning of birth,

But fail to mention our time here on earth,

You entice us with beauty, money and fame,

But leave us all empty from the things that we gain,

From you, grow flowers, plants and trees,

But also comes thorns and poisonous things,

You appear so kind and gentle at first,

But behind you is death full of hunger and thirst,

Oh life, how can you dare be so cruel?,

My hope in you now has turned me a fool,

Your mouth speaks of wars, famine and lies,

But your ugliness has shown, no longer disguised,

I now see you for how you were meant to be,

A short walk on my path towards eternity

LIGHTS, CAMERA, ACTION!

The time has come and this is my moment,

No turning back now, I have to own it,

So many lights on stage, nearly blinding me,

I look out into the crowd, but I still can't see,

Do I remember my lines? Wait, I forgot a word,

I'll just improvise since no one has heard,

How do I look? Is my makeup right?,

Can the crowd see my pimple up under the light?,

My hair is a mess, but it's too late now,

When the show is over, should I take a bow?,

Or should I just curtsy and wave my hand?,

Will an encore be what the crowd demands?,

Should I stand stage left or is it stage right?,

I think center stage has the best light,

Am I loud enough? Or maybe I'm too loud,

Do you think my performance will make them proud?,

I wonder who all came to see my show,

Will they all stay afterwards or decide to just go?,

Do I change my wardrobe after this scene?,

Or was it before this one? The dress should've been green,

Did I grab the prop that was on top of the table?,

I was suppose to say steeple, but instead I said staple!,

The show is almost over, just a few more lines,

If I mess up now do you think they'll mind?,

Wait, the curtains are closing! Did I say my part?,

Will they now appreciate my love for the art?,

I worked hard for this moment, this is my passion,

Well, on to the next scene, Lights, Camera, Action!

LOVE

I never realized what it was like to love until I understood hate,

I mean you can't have one without the other right, at least that's what they say,

Sometimes I love you and other times I can't stand you,

But it never should escalate to the point where your face is black and blue,

You see, I was never able to comprehend how these two things worked together,

Because I thought that when you said that you loved someone the love lasted forever,

I guess it's true, love is only a four letter word until it transforms into action,

To some it means more wrote in a Hallmark card especially in big captions,

Some use love as a weapon it poisons you quicker than saying, "I hate you!,"

Some use love in exchange for sex only later to degrade you,

So how can you be in love with someone if you have never experienced it firsthand?

People think that they can obtain it with gifts and compliments on demand,

But you see love is more than a four-letter word it's more of a verb than a noun,

And people they search all over the world for love, but for some its nowhere to be found,

You see so many people getting a divorce, cheating or beating up their wives,

Now if you can't love yourself how are you going to make a deposit into someone else's life?

You hear people say that they "fell in love," but really they just "failed to love,"

Because no one truly understands that definition except the one who created it up above,

The Bible says, "Love is patient, it's kind, it does not envy, it does not boast, it's not proud,"

But it takes more than reading about it in the good book or quoting scriptures out loud,

Love is about forgiving and doing what's right instead of wrong,

Cause you see the first sign of love I ever heard about, was mocked, beaten, and crucified to a cross all alone,

So, think before you tell someone you love them, or you may just have to pay a price,

Cause you see, to some love is an addiction, if you play with their heart, they might take your life,

Now I don't know about you, but that's definitely not the type of love I crave,

So don't get caught in society's definition of love, or you'll soon become it's slave!

MAKE A DIFFERENCE

Did you know that you make a difference in each one of your students' lives?,

The things you think to them don't matter, you may actually be surprised,

You're not just educators preparing them for graduation,

Some look up to you as parents something far beyond education,

So don't hold your head down when you feel like you aren't getting through,

Just when you think they're not paying attention, they're actually listening to you,

It's not always by what you say, but it's your actions that stand on out,

And trust me, when they get older it's definitely you they'll remember without a doubt,

Teachers are so important, but they don't get a lot of recognition,

They help lead kids down the righteous path and encourage them to make good decisions,

It's not just about learning how to write or finding the answer to math equations,

A lot of teachers show students how to respect with little to no persuasion,

You teach them how to wait their turns and raise their hand when they have something to say,

You show them discipline, structure and love while teaching them how to obey,

You help build their confidence and show them how to work as a team,

And if you think that doesn't make a difference, you help boost their self-esteem,

Some students want to go to college because you give them inspiration,

Some become doctors, lawyers or nurses or because of your motivation,

They see the love that you have for them and want them to do their best,

And because of you they become successful because of the time you chose to invest,

So quit worrying about if you're making a difference because you had a bad day in class,

Just know that teachers are the reasons why occupations are able to last,

Without our teachers we wouldn't be able to learn how to do our jobs,

And I know sometimes you may feel unappreciated and that your time has been robbed,

But just know that what you do for them is far beyond what money can buy,

And the next time someone asks you why you teach, please remember these reasons why,

Your role goes far beyond the classroom and well beyond what you can see,

Because to be a teacher is more than just a job and everything that I aspire to be!

ME TOO

I was afraid to speak out for fear I would be judged,

The looks of disapproval, suspicious glances, or curious minds

wondering why I didn't say, "no,"

Those demons bottled up inside of me whispering lies in my ear,

"You liked it!" "You wanted this to happen!" or "You could've

just left!"

I've played this blame game on more occasions than I could

count,

Replaying each situation in my mind, calculating at which point I

"could've, should've, or would've" but didn't, do this or that,

I've even questioned my own mentality, labeling myself as crazy,

stupid, or gullible,

I despised the word "victim" because that made me seem weak

and pathetic,

But in reality I was a "victim," I was helpless in those situations,

Trapped by his body of lies, threats, and manipulations,

My voice muffled by his groans and grunts as his filthy sweat

poured over me,

Each time it happened the little girl died inside,

My innocence blotted out by my blood stained sheets,

Every secret and detail of those assaults were hidden in my

mattress,

But, I couldn't tell anyone because who would believe a child?

Or maybe they knew, but just chose to ignore those unwarranted assaults,

Making me pay for a debt that I didn't owe,

I wanted to end my pain, or end his on many occasions, but I didn't have the strength,

I just allowed it to happen, over and over again,

With nowhere to run and hide, or no one to protect me,

That same scared, little girl now faces that same situation,

But this time his face is different, younger but just as scary,

His eyes are piercing with malice, his grip just as strong, but cautious,

I want to scream, but I'm afraid I will only put myself in more danger,

I want to fight back, but he outweighs me at least by 30 pounds or more,

So I just lay there and allow him to do what I've always allowed them to do to me,

Ignoring the pain, stifling my screams, and praying that it's over just as fast as it started,

My innocence being taken away from me again like it was the first time,

My heart is racing, I hear all of those slurs spewing out at me, "whore" and "slut,"

I know that I can't come forward because I've already been labeled by them,

They've already judged me without knowing the dirty little details,

I'm a victim, but yet, my failure to run or fight back puts me at fault, or at least partially to blame,

So when I hear those stories of unsolicited attacks,

Countless women who've been sexually abused, taken advantage of, or harassed,

I don't stand up, but I quietly whisper to myself "me too."

MENTAL HEALTH

"She's just crazy, you know she's been that way for years,"

"I don't know why she always brings that drama over here,"

"Acting like she's all depressed, but you know it's just an act,"

"I'm so tired of everyone always cutting her some slack,"

These type of labels are what people have to face every day,

Their mental health is disregarded and their problems are turned away,

They're labeled as crazy, dramatic or overly sensitive,

When what they really need is for someone to sit down and listen,

Everyday lives are lost by suicide from depression,

But how many of those lives could've been saved through intervention?,

We are so quick to judge without knowing all of the facts,

Mental health is real so please don't assume it's just an act,

When we see someone smiling we may think that they're fine,

But that smile could be covering up those demons inside,

We don't know what others go through on a day to day basis,

Anxiety, depression and bipolar disorder have many faces,

These are just some common disorders, but there are more on the list,

So don't ignore anyone's problems just because their symptoms don't fit,

A smile, hug, or conversation just might help them get through,

Sometimes medication is necessary from a doctor's point of view,

Mental health is a serious issue we all face every day,

Some struggle more than others just to get through the day,

It could be your mom, dad, friend or even yourself,

So please be considerate when talking about someone's mental health!

MISSING YOU

Walking into your room that day,

It made my blood turn cold,

You weren't suppose to die yet,

At least not til' you were old,

I didn't want to believe it,

I just hugged you last night,

Who would take care of us now?

And make sure that we're alright,

You just laid there in silence,

You didn't blink or bat an eye,

My hands softly touched your body,

As tears poured from my eyes,

How could you be gone so soon?

And just leave us both behind,

Were you even sad to leave us?

What thoughts ran through your mind?

You were my mom, yet my friend,

Your life was snatched away so quick,

No more pancakes in the morning,

No more hugs when we were sick,

No more dancing in the hallway,

No more sleeping in your bed,

No more polish on your nails,

No more rollers on your head,

No more trips to the laundry mat,

No more helping you fold clothes,

No more combing our pretty hair,

No more making us wear bows,

How could this happen to an angel?

Who was loved and held so dear,

The very absence of your presence,

Makes me wish that you were here,

I know that you were suffering,

And God granted you eternal rest

He returned one of his angels,

Because He always knows what's best.

If I could have another day with you,

I'd cherish that moment til the end,

But for now, rest in peace mommy,

And I hope to see you then.

MONDAY

I use to hate to see you coming, my least favorite day of the week,

If I could've traded you for another day, Friday would've been mine to keep,

You use to make my workdays busy, always causing a lot of stress,

Even driving there was a headache and traffic was always a mess,

The weekends would fly by quickly, but you would take your precious time,

If there are twenty four hours in a day, why did it take you forty nine?,

I couldn't wait for you to be over so I could see another day,

If I could've skipped through days of the week, I would've landed on Wednesday,

At least that day is not as busy because it's the middle of the week,

Some people even call it "Humpday" to celebrate getting over the peak,

But now, I look at you differently, I no longer hold a grudge,

You're the start of a new beginning so it's not my place to judge,

I look forward to seeing you coming, I now embrace you with a smile,

So cheers to you, Monday, I will see you after a while.

MOTHER

Mother's Day is coming and as I sit back and think about all of the gifts that I could buy for you, I'll gift you instead with this poem,

When I hear the word "mother" it hits me deeper than the regular definition you find in the dictionary,

You see, I lost my mother when I was eight, but make no mistake that you were, is and are a "mother" to me,

And I don't take the word, "mother" lightly,

The role of a mother is to not only protect and nurture her children,

But to also teach them about resilience,

And that's exactly what you taught me,

You fought for me day and night through your prayers,

And although you came in when we were halfway grown, you stripped down many of my layers,

You taught me how to love someone who wasn't exactly your own,

And you made a house that wasn't yours into a home,

And for that I say, "thank you,"

Although my own mother was taken from me, you still had enough love to step in and claim me,

So that's why I no longer look at you as my stepmother,

It took me a while to recover, but through this broken heart you

helped me to discover love again,

You became not only my mother, but my friend,

You coached me through sports and made it simple,

Taught me all of basketball's fundamentals,

How to shoot a layup, play defense, post up and run a play,

And you coached me through life and now I'm a mother today,

"Thank you"

You not only prepared hot delicious meals and baked moist

buttery cakes,

But you made sure that every day we sat as a family and ate,

You taught me how to perm and curl my hair,

Things that I learned from you, but you may not have been aware,

You taught me how push when I got tired,

Even though my lungs felt expired,

You were there to inspire,

You told me to keep running and finish the race with all that I

had,

Showed me how to love others through the good, ugly and bad,

And that's why today I'm so glad for you, mother,

Although you didn't give birth to me, you still gave birth in me,

Planted those seeds of "I could be anything I wanted to be,"

You see, I never told you just how grateful I am for you,

How your love found me and guided me through,

Even on my darkest days you knew just what I needed,

A word, your prayers in which you seeded into my spirit,

At times I didn't want to hear it, but you gave me the truth even when I feared it,

You showed me how to face my problems head on,

Handled me with love even when I was dead wrong,

So, I not only write this for you, but I sing this song,

"Mother, I thank God for you!,"

Who would have ever known that the mother that I had lost came back though the tears I've cried and watered the seeds you've sown?,

Mother,

So, I can now say it to you with so much conviction, my tongue no longer has restrictions, my heart beats no longer conflicted,

Mother,

Your seeds helped me bloom into who I am today,

No greater words could I mutter from my heart and say, but that "I love you" and "Happy Mother's Day!"

MOTHER'S DAY

Why do we call it Mother's Day when our roles remain the same?,

We are not just mothers on that day, having children earned us that name,

There is more to being a mother than what meets the standard eye,

Giving birth is just a part of it, but what we do no money can buy,

We are nurtures, caregivers, and we love unconditionally,

We are chefs, nurses, bakers, and are the heart of our families,

We are housekeepers and stylist we make sure you look your best,

We are tutors and teachers, we prepare you for your tests,

We are accountants and secretaries, we make sure you stay on track,

We are chauffeurs and chaperones, always watching over your back,

Being a mother is not just a title that we carry so lightly,

We put ourselves last for our families, and do things rightly,

We are detectives when you lose things or can't find your favorite toy,

We are the planners for family vacations making sure you all enjoy,

Being a mother is not a holiday to spend money on expensive presents,

Our greatest gift is the love you give us and embracing us with your lovely presence,

So give us flowers while we're here and don't take our love in vain,

Mother's Day is what we call it, but a mother we'll always remain

MY CLOSET

I need to clean out my closet, but I don't want you to see,

Everything inside there that's not suppose to be,

I'm trying my best to close it so that none of it spills out,

But my closet's just too full so I have no other route,

I had no other choice what else was I suppose to do?,

I didn't want to use yours and overwhelm you too,

There's so much hidden in there that I didn't want to share,

I know you have your own stuff and probably wouldn't care,

I don't know what's all in there, but I can tell it won't be long,

Before my mess's exposed and you see what doesn't belong,

I need to clean out my closet, but I need a little help,

Normally I wouldn't ask, but I can't do it by myself,

I know you have your own mess, but mine is getting worse,

The stuff I hid inside there has now began to hurt,

My closet's way too full for me to pretend it doesn't exist,

There's a lot I stored inside, too much to go down the list,

I need to clean out my closet, I can now no longer wait,

Before it all consumes me and by then it'll be too late!

NEVER LET YOU GO

Laying on the table with tear-stained eyes,

My heart beating rapidly, mind full of why's,

I never meant to hurt you, that's what I want to say,

No matter how much I loved you, I knew you couldn't stay,

The choices I have made, led me to this moment,

No one's fault but mine, so this decision I will own it,

Counting back the days, I first knew of your existence,

Fear clouded my mind, this decision I couldn't resist it,

The last moments of your life, now snatched away,

Tears rolling down my eyes, no words are left to say,

Into thin air you vanish, a vapor yet a life,

My mind full of regret, heart beating with strife,

Now the deed is done, hands of time can't be reversed,

Empty womb full of sorrow, crying lips slightly pursed,

I hope to see you one day, so I can let you know,

If I had enough courage, I would have never let you go!

NON-DISCLOSURE

For seven years I felt secure in my own bubble,

You not knowing my whereabouts gave me the power to be free,

I felt like I could truly live without the threat of your presence lurking around my neighborhood, job, or me taking trips to the store,

I could walk around and pretend that you didn't exist because for seven years, you didn't,

Looking out of my window was nothing more than just seeing what the neighbors across the street were doing,

I can still see that dent in the middle of the blinds,

A quiet reminder of the freedom to just observe without fear,

To be able to watch without being watched,

Walking to my car in the middle of the night didn't alarm me,

Although I naturally checked my back seat, it was more out of habit than the thought of you waiting to catch me off guard,

My level of awareness was at an all-time low because I knew the risk was minimal,

Unfortunately, my security has been breached by the dismissal of a non-disclosure of my address,

It caught me off guard in the way that someone who is casually walking down the sidewalk and gets struck by a car is caught off guard,

You feel safe and protected on that slab of concrete, oblivious to the fact that a car would be able to break that barrier of protection,

For seven years, I was untouchable, unreachable, and undetectable,

But now, my level of awareness is at an all-time high,

My once, "casually peaking though the blinds" has turned into, "Is he out there?" or "Who's car is that?,"

The paranoia that has crept in the back of my mind of your unwelcome visits,

The days get a little shorter and the nights become longer,

I tell myself that I'm no longer afraid of you,

Your stature, although great, is nothing more than a shell disguising the coward who lives inside,

The hands that once hurt me are nothing but dead weight holding on to empty threats,

Those eyes that once stared at me so menacingly, are blinded by the truth that I've moved on,

Your manipulative words that once had power over me, are nothing more than a cry for help,

I actually pity you, you thought that you could control me forever,

Your old threats are drowned out by my refusal to allow you to dictate my life,

I thought that I needed a non-disclosure, but I understand now that you need it more than I do,

Because we both know that your lack of maturity, your inability to control your emotions has landed you exactly where you didn't think you'd be,

Alone.

OH, THAT YOU WOULD BLESS ME LORD

Oh, that you would bless me Lord,

Each and every day,

At times my soul gets weary,

Don't let your hand astray,

Lead me on my journey,

So that I may follow you,

Help me see the good Lord,

In everything that you do,

Open up my eyes Lord,

And let me see your light,

Carry me up the mountain,

To see life from your sight,

Hold me a little closer,

And never put me down,

Lift my burdens from me,

And place them on the ground,

Rock me in your arms Lord,

And put me on to sleep,

Guide me through the night Lord,

And cover me with your peace,

Wake me in the morning,

With a sweet, gentle touch,

Help me show the world Lord,

That you love them very much,

Cover me in your presence,

Lift me from the sinking sand,

Help me not to ever,

Let go of your precious hand!

ONE DAY

You visit me very often, but each time it's not the same,

Some days you leave me breathless, other times you cause me pain,

I sit around and wonder what I've ever done to you,

To make me feel all alone and not knowing what to do,

You tell me all of your lies and watch me shiver from the fear,

And whisper, "You're going to die" while laughing closely by my ear,

I try to count to ten while beads of sweat drip down my face,

Or take a long, long walk as my mind begins to race,

You never show me mercy, it's intense each time we meet,

My mouth becomes real dry and makes it hard for me to speak,

But one day I'm coming for you, you'll see a different side of me,

And you'll no longer be known as my anxiety!

PAINKILLERS

They say laughter is the best medicine, but then why am I still in pain?

They say Advil can ease your hurt, but you have to take it again and again,

And then they make all of these prescription drugs, to numb the pain you feel,

But in reality it deceives you from what is fake and real,

From Advil to Tylenol, Vicodin to Oxycontin,

None of these cure anything, none can solve your problems,

People depend on these drugs to cope with their pain,

So, they lie, they steal, they kill, they do whatever it takes to gain,

Because they are addicted to a fantasy while reality waits for revenge,

Lost in another world, being high their only friend,

Abandoning family and friends to live a life all alone,

Blinded by another world, helpless on their own,

Doctors are getting rich while the sick are steady dying,

Writing prescriptions after prescriptions, lost souls are steady buying,

Confused about their lives broken dreams are shattered,

Overdosing off painkillers as if they never mattered,

Painkillers, yeah that's what they call them because that is exactly what they do,

They deceive you from reality and take the lives of you!

PATIENCE

Patience is a seed beginning to grow,

Watered and nurtured, tilled and sowed,

Patience is a plant that transforms into a tree,

A jar of honey created by a hive of bees,

Patience is a caterpillar that becomes a butterfly,

A baby bird preparing to one day fly,

Patience is a cake baking in the oven,

A pile of straw for a basket that's carefully woven,

Patience is a bruise starting to heal,

A chef in the kitchen preparing a meal,

Patience is trusting in God's holy word,

While waiting for an answer you still haven't heard,

Patience builds faith and eases troubled minds,

And without it, peace is often hard to find!

QUARANTINE

We are warned to stay at home to calm the spread of this disease,

But yet, some choose to ignore the request and still go out as they please,

They think the flu is far more harmful people die from every year,

And that the Covid is way less scary so they walk around without a fear,

We are told to wear a mask to protect us from infected air,

And to wash our hands for twenty seconds and scrub with soap for extra care,

Many stores around the country are running out of their supplies,

People hurrying to the stores to see what's left that they can buy,

Some people are forced to work from home while other's lives are put at risk,

Stimulus checks are being deposited to aid this economic hit,

Smaller businesses are shutting down while other ones are bailing out,

Different companies are laying off or looking for another route,

School is taught through distance learning from the comforts of our home,

Graduations are being cancelled; seniors wondering what's going on,

Young and old are steady dying from this disease every day,

Ten or less allowed at funerals to send their loved ones on their way,

People risk their health and others just to be out on the scene,

But all of this could've been avoided if only they chose to quarantine!

REFLECTION

I use to be afraid to look in the mirror because the person staring back was embarrassing to see,

I use to be afraid to look in the mirror disappointed of the image who looked like me,

I use to be afraid to look in the mirror unable to speak kind words to myself,

I use to be afraid to look in the mirror ashamed of the thoughts inside I felt,

I use to be afraid to look in the mirror unworthy of the love my presence ran away,

I use to be afraid to look in the mirror angry at that person who stood in the way,

I use to be afraid to look in the mirror until self-worth reached out and kissed my face,

I use to be afraid to look in the mirror until love wrapped me up in it's warm embrace,

I use to be afraid to look in the mirror until forgiveness stared back and smiled at me,

I use to be afraid to look in the mirror until confidence reached out it's hand to me,

I use to be afraid to look in the mirror because I thought it was

for my own protection,

Now I'm not afraid to look in the mirror because

I see the beauty in my reflection.

SILENCE

We needed you to speak up for us, but you remained silent,

Your words unsaid provoked anger within us, that could have been extinguished with just three simple words, "I'm with you,"

We said that "Black Lives Matter" but it wasn't that we thought that we were more superior,

We just wanted to be included, to feel a part of this United States of America,

We were suppose to be one nation under God, but the division has proved that we are not indivisible,

There is no liberty because we do not have justice for all,

We have witnessed the hypocrisy in this country,

It's more offensive to kneel during the National Anthem, than it is to kneel on someone's neck and squeeze the very life out of them,

"I can't breathe"

The very words pled by a dying man,

The average amount of time it takes to sing the National Anthem is under two minutes,

"Oh, say can you see" George Floyd's neck being kneeled on for almost nine,

"By the dawn's early light" Ahmaud Arbery was gunned down outside while out for a jog,

"What so proudly we hailed" eight bullets into Breonna Taylor as she lay their sleeping, "at the twilight's last gleaming,"

"I can't breathe"

Your silence speaks volumes far beyond the screams of protesters,

We needed you to stand up for us, but for years you remained hidden,

Tucked away in your comfortable homes, safely behind your keyboards,

Judging the videos of unjustified murders like you were a judge on America's Got Talent,

And we all know who won first place, the American Idols,

"I can't breathe"

Even though his very breath was seeping away from his lungs he still had enough courage to cry out,

But yet, you sit there with lungs full of air and choose to cower behind your silence,

"I can't breathe"

It seems like the Declaration of Independence was rewritten,

"We hold these truths to be self-evident, that all men are created equal, but they will not be treated as equal, that they are endowed by their Creator with certain unalienable rights unless you are Black, Brown, or other minorities, that among these are life unless we fear for ours and take yours away, liberty until they get thrown in jail for 20 plus years for non-violent crimes, and the pursuit of happiness as long as it's not interfering with our happiness"

"I can't breathe"

How many times must our breath be taken away from us before you use yours to speak out?,

"Hands up don't shoot"

Your silence pierces through our exposed bodies,

Your bullet proof words could've been used to shield us from these injustices,

But yet, you chose silence, and allowed us to die alone,

America the Beautiful, but yet your ugliness has shown,

Time and time again, brown and black bodies have been used as bricks to build a wall we can't seem to tear down,

A wall of racism, hate, and inequality that has been standing for over 400 years,

Rosa Parks refused to give up her seat to racism,

So that Dr. Martin Luther King, Jr. could have his dream that "one day our nation would rise up and live out the true meaning of its creed,"

But his dream has turned into a nightmare for brown and black people,

An American Horror Story for all to see while they "Netflix and chill" doing absolutely nothing about it,

"I can't breathe"

Our bodies are being exchanged for hashtags, our faces are being printed on t-shirts, and our last words are being retweeted faster than the videos of our deaths are being circulated,

"We can't breathe"

Our race shouldn't be our crime,

Our skin shouldn't be our sin,

But until you join the fight and speak up for us, your silence will continue to kill us faster than any bullet can.

SOCIAL MEDIA

It's right at your fingertips everything you want to see,

Slowly drawing you in to a fake reality,

You see your favorite celebrities living the dream,

But everything you view isn't always what it seems,

They show off their perfect bodies and claim it's fantastic,

It looks real online, but behind doors made of plastic,

You start believing the lie that this world has created,

The once normal life you lived all of sudden is now hated,

Young girls start believing they should look a certain way,

Their self-esteem is lowered as they are steady led astray,

Young boys are shown that they should have a lot of women,

So they don't value relationships in order to fit in,

People start living well beyond their means,

All to live a life as they see upon the screen,

Influencers are paid to promote things online,

People hurrying to stores to see what they can find,

Celebrities are so attached to this fancy way of living,

People selling their souls to get what they're getting,

Society is flocking behind these wolves like sheep,

Trying to maintain what they can't afford to keep,

They say the devil wears Prada, but you choose to ignore,

You depreciate your life so that you can have more,

Social media is used to distract us from the scene,

But everything you see isn't always what it seems.

SORRY

Mama

He said that he was "sorry" and begged me not to leave,

I know that he can change if only I believe,

He pushed me to the ground, but I know it was my fault,

At least he didn't hit me because then that'd be assault,

He grabbed me by the arm and left a little bruise,

At least it isn't broken because then that'd be abuse,

He squeezed my throat real tight, but let go before I fell,

At least I didn't pass out because then he'd be in jail,

He slapped me in the face but it only hurt awhile,

At least we were alone and not in front of our child,

He threw a bottle at me but thank God he barely missed,

At least he didn't hit me with it balled up in his fist,

He pulled a gun on me, but he didn't squeeze the trigger,

He was trying to make a point at least that's what I figure,

He hit my head against the wall and made me break my nose,

He blamed it on the alcohol, it was an accident I suppose,

Today he said he'd kill me, but I know he's just real mad,

He told me that he's "sorry" so that outweighs the bad,

Child

I'm hiding in the closet because I just heard mama scream,

I can hear dad yelling at her about some stupid little thing,

He told her that he'd kill her, but she didn't call the cops,

Now I hear a crash as mama begs for him to stop,

I can't get out of the closet because I'm too afraid to help,

I want to protect mama but I can't do it by myself,

I hear a real loud bang, but this time mama didn't scream,

I don't hear daddy either, I guess he's done, at least it seems,

I walk out of the closet to look for mama in her room,

But I don't see her there, she must be in the kitchen I assume,

I walk into the kitchen and find mama on the floor,

But something isn't right, she looks different than before,

I say her name real loud, but she doesn't move at all,

When I get a little closer, I see blood upon the tile,

I run over to the phone and quickly dial 9-1-1,

But by the time the cops arrive mama is already gone.

SPRING

Your sweet nectar is satisfying to my tongue,

Just as bread is fulfilling to the poor,

I breathe in your very presence,

Such a sweet aroma to my nostrils,

You look at me as if for the first time,

Awed and amazed by my beauty,

You reach for my hand and gently brush my fingertips,

A wave of ecstasy jolts your body and lights up your soul,

Our past, present and future unfolds before your eyes,

Love is the seed and our hearts are the soil,

Let it grow and blossom as flowers do in the spring.

STAND FOR SOMETHING

It's so easy to laugh and point fingers when we ourselves are not in pain,

Often times we turn our backs, when a reward is not the gain,

But aren't we just as guilty, as the ones who commit the crime?,

Turning ourselves into judges suggesting how they'll do their time,

Why aren't we taking a stand when we see others doing wrong?

Instead of encouraging one another, we choose to leave them all alone,

Blaming the victim for their fate, as we are steady led astray,

Turning deaf ears to our brothers, no kind words will we say,

Watching others get in trouble while we just steady pass them by,

Searching for answers to our problems when we are the reason why,

So don't just fall for anything, and decide to do nothing,

Be courageous and speak up, but most of all stand for something!

STRESS

The kids are acting up, and all of my bills are due,

Refrigerator's empty, I'm out of groceries too,

I had it up to here, with all of this stress,

Only one source of income to help me with this mess,

What am I to do with all of these crazy bills?,

Am I the only one who understands how this feels?,

Sick and tired of bill collectors blowing up my phone,

I don't have any money so please leave me alone,

Tired and worn out from working all day long,

I come home to a mess, everything is going wrong,

Somebody please help me, and get me out of this mess,

So I can have a peace of mind from all of this stress!

TEXAS

They say that everything is bigger and better in Texas,

And I must say, I agree,

I'm not being biased just because I was raised here,

Just look around and you will see,

If you look at the US map, it's hard to miss us because we stand out,

There's no way to mistake us for another state,

Our presence leaves no room for doubt,

We have big animals, farms, houses and trucks to a few,

And have you seen the size of our mosquitoes, they're almost bigger than a shoe,

Texas has so much land, it takes half a day to drive across,

By the time you reach the other side, you would've almost gotten lost,

We love chili, bluebonnets, rodeos and wear cowboy boots with big straw hats,

We have pecan trees, bass fish, mockingbirds and our soil is Houston black,

We love playing the guitar, singing country music and fishing at the lake,

But be careful if you decide to go camping, you just might run across a rattlesnake,

We're known as the "friendly state" and always greet our visitors with a smile,

And if you ever had a home cooked meal from here then you've been blessed with southern style,

We have oil rigs, cattle, shopping malls and play Texas 42 dominoes,

There's not a person who doesn't know who we are, our name precedes us wherever we go,

I'm just a lady raised in Texas, y'all don't have to take a word from me,

I've given you the reasons why our state is great, but "bless your heart" if y'all can't see!

THE BOUQUET

If I could give you flowers, I'd arrange the most beautiful bouquet,

And they would represent you in their own special way,

Roses would symbolize the eternal love you left behind,

I'd add a Daisy for you mama because you were one of a kind,

Chrysanthemums would go in next because you gave us so much joy,

Add in Tulips for the happy years we all were blessed to enjoy,

Gardenias for the grief we felt the day you went away,

Put in Lilies for the pure love you gave us each and every day,

Daffodils because I hope to be half of the mother you were to us,

Throw in Carnations for the gratitude from all of the lives that you've touched,

Orchids for the grace you showed to others all around,

Delphiniums to represent the new experiences in life you found,

Lavender to symbolize your sweet, calm and gentle soul,

Then I'd place them in a jar with a big, beautiful bow,

I'd deliver them to you myself to see the smile upon your face,

And tell you how much I love you and that you could never be replaced,

I know you're no longer here, but your presence is still felt every day,

And I'll always keep your memory alive through flowers arranged in a bouquet

Alicia S. Azahar

THE CASUAL HELLO

You called me just to say "hello,"

but we both know that isn't true,

Your "hello" expired ten minutes ago,

your time is well past due,

You forgot how well I know your ways,

no innocence here I've found,

The lonely nights you spend at home,

won't make me come around,

You've kept your distance for a while,

but here you are at last,

Whispering sweet nothings in my ear,

hoping you'll get a pass,

But trust me when I tell you,

my "goodbye" is all you'll know,

Forever embedded in your heart,

full of your empty "hellos"

THE DAY BEFORE CHRISTMAS

It was the day before Christmas and all through the town,

People were shopping and rushing around,

Sale signs were hung on the store fronts with care,

Hoping that shoppers soon would be there,

Parents were flustered from the list that they read,

While visions of empty shelves danced in their heads,

I in my car, with my purse on my lap,

Had just stopped at Flying Squirrel for an afternoon snack,

When all through the streets there arose such a clatter,

I dropped my muffin mid bite to see what was the matter,

I opened the car door as quick as a flash,

And jumped on the sidewalk to investigate the crash,

The sun beamed hot on us all down below,

As we hurried around to witness the show,

When suddenly to my curious eyes should appear,

But a man dressed in red holding a large can of beer,

For a second, I thought it was this man that was hit,

This poor, knock off version of our dear old St. Nick,

Quicker than lightening the town people came,

As he shouted and laughed and called some by name,

Hey, Catherine! Hi Danny! Amy and Vincent,

Juan, Violet, Sean, Susan, John, Sandra, and Winston,

Let's go eat at The Porch and after shop at the mall,

Now drive away, drive away, drive away you all!,

As a house in a Texas tornado sure flies,

The man disappeared right in front of my eyes,

What was once a large crowd, now left but a few,

With their cars loaded down with new toys and new shoes,

And then I heard jingling on top of a roof,

As I saw Christmas lights come unraveled and loose,

Like a deer in headlights, I turned my head right around,

And discovered a bag full of toys on the ground,

I snatched up the bag like a pirate with loot,

And rushed back to the store quickly on foot,

With the bundle of toys hanging over my back,

I asked for the store manager who was fixing a rack,

His eyes sparkled bright and his voice was real merry,

With snow colored hair and cheeks redder than cherries,

His small, pouty mouth formed an inverted rainbow,

With a beard full of hair like a mountain of snow,

The blunt end of a pen, he held with his teeth,

With papers in hand and a clipboard beneath,

He had a soft round face and a big 'ol belly,

That jiggled when he laughed like a pile of grape jelly,

Such a plump old man almost big as a shelf,

I let out a chuckle at the sight to myself,

The look in his eyes as he tilted his head,

Made me pause in my tracks as I heard what he said,

He spoke just few words before he turned back to work,

"You can keep all of those toys you found on the curb,"

In shock, I just stood there, my mouth wouldn't close,

As I thought to myself, "how could he possibly know?",

He called to his staff with a hoot and a whistle,

As I sprang out the store like a bullet in a pistol,

I heard him cry out as I ran out of sight,

"Merry Christmas tomorrow and have a good night!"

THE PILLOW

I often cry myself to sleep allowing my tears to saturate your presence,

Your soft, gentle assurance presses closely against my face,

Collecting my tears one by one, drip by drip, and moan by moan,

Sometimes my angry screams are stifled by your feathered casing,

Capturing those curses meant to reach bending ears,

I hug you ever so tightly, slowly suffocating my fears,

You never put up a fight, allowing my anxiety to melt into your body,

Calmness showers down on me, rocking me to sleep in your gentle arms,

I'm one with you, my dreams seep out through my cold sweat,

Whispering past secrets and future aspirations, that only you know,

Trust is your greatest possession, my words and thoughts are your prisoners,

Your familiar nature seeks no betrayal with me,

And there is nothing more reassuring than you,

my greatest sanctuary!

THE SCAR

I use to hate looking in the mirror at you,

Your ugliness staring back at me, taunting me each day,

That permanent indention right underneath my belly button,

Reminding me that I couldn't have a natural birth,

You weren't even cut the normal way along my bikini line,

At least that would've hidden you from my view,

I would often hear all of these jokes about you, further fueling my disgust,

Making me feel less than a woman because I couldn't do what so many other women have been able to,

Why wasn't I able to give birth the natural way?

How come I was left with such an ugly reminder of my failure?,

I use to be so embarrassed to wear a two piece bathing suit because I knew your appearance would cause people to stare,

Curious eyes glancing over my physique and suddenly pausing as they discovered your ugliness lingering there,

I've even had other women question why I had to be cut open in this odd way,

The shame that would wash over me because I was left to explain something so personal to strangers,

Although it wasn't their business, I felt the need to explain your existence,

Because at least then people would have some sort of understanding,

I hated you because my stomach no longer looked the same,

All of the scar tissue developing over the years underneath you,

Causing my stomach to puff up and have this weird pudge at the bottom,

No matter how many sit-ups I did, I still couldn't get rid of this new stomach you created,

My insecurities stuck out like a sore thumb just as you did every time I put on a dress,

Although people would tell me how good I looked in it,

I still felt your presence underneath my clothes tormenting me,

Because I still looked as though I was expecting,

But, throughout the years I've developed an appreciation for you,

I remember the day of my daughter's birth,

How quickly everything escalated as I tried to push her out of me,

My heart rate rising and just as quickly hers too,

I remember the nurse raising her voice and telling me that I needed to hurry up and push this baby out of me,

My daughter was in "distress" and it was only getting worse,

For some reason I just couldn't get her passed my birth canal,

"Why wouldn't she budge?"

They even placed a mirror at the foot of the bed for me to see the progress or lack thereof,

I remember the guilt and fear I felt because what mother wants to be the cause of a life threatening situation for her baby?,

They rolled me into the operating room and a doctor came in with a needle of anesthesia,

I was asked to count down from ten, but I don't think I made it past nine,

Lights out, darkness poured over me like a storm cloud,

I've never experienced death, but I could only imagine that it felt like that very moment,

Dark, black nothingness,

At the time they did what they thought was necessary and performed an emergency cesarean,

I woke up from what seemed like an eternity in another room,

They rolled my daughter inside so that I could see her,

I remember gazing at her beautiful face and holding her in my arms,

The fear that I had before seeped out of me as I inhaled her sweet fragrance,

She was worth it,

That ugly reminder of what I thought was my failure was actually a beautiful reminder of the life I was allowed to create,

A life that I was allowed to carry for nine months,

A life that was intended to be here and not perish,

A beautiful life that came from something I once thought was so ugly.

THINK BEFORE YOU SPEAK

They say there's power in the tongue so be careful what you say,

Life or death is the wager, choose the price you want to pay,

It doesn't take a lot of effort to think twice before you speak,

Just because your choice is silence it doesn't make you frail or weak,

I would rather stand in silence than use my words to stir up anger,

You never know when your mouth could lead you to a trail of danger,

Walk away from that fight, allow peace to ease your mind,

But if trouble is what you seek then it won't be hard to find,

Sticks and stones may break your bones, but words internally will cause a bruise,

So before you start to speak be clear of the words you choose,

It's up to you to take the high road even if it causes pain,

You have a lot more to lose than you would ever have to gain.

TO THE BIC KIDS

You are not what they say you are so don't listen to the lies,

When you look into the mirror what do you see through your eyes?

Are you a problem? A disruption? Do you lack respect for others?

Or is there something deeper inside you that you're afraid to discover?

When I look across the room I see bright futures and success,

I see young women and men who just want to be the best,

Have you made a few mistakes? Sure! Who hasn't in their life?,

But it's what you learn from those mistakes in which you can apply,

You may have been labeled as angry, but turn that anger into a smile,

Instead of using your words to tear down, lift your peers out of the pile,

Listen to your parents and allow your teachers to guide you through,

They are only there to help and bring the best out of you,

Don't carry those labels as a burden because it's not yours to bear,

Instead drop them on the ground and show the world how much you care,

Surround yourself with others who influence you in a positive way,

Remember, actions speak louder than words, but still be careful what you say,

You have the power to change the world no matter what others think of you,

But it's up to you to decide what path in life you want to choose!

TRANSFORMATION

Take a look at your life and decide what you want to be,

Do you want to live in excellence or in mediocrity?

You have to transform your mind to fit the path you want to take,

Being excellent comes with a price from the choices that you make,

Take advantage of your life by applying these values every day,

Set your goals with clear vision, remove distractions out of your way,

Hold yourself accountable and don't make excuses when you fall,

Live your life on purpose and everyday give your all,

Change isn't easy, but you will be grateful in the end,

So why wait until tomorrow for your transformation to begin?

UNTIL THE INK RUNS DRY

My words and thoughts pour out from you,

Carefully displaying my inner true self,

You record my truths unapologetically

Delivering each stroke with purpose,

There are no judgements being cast down,

Your key unlocks my mind from imprisonment,

Exposed and open, I dare not hide my vulnerability,

I'm protected from misconstrued speculations,

Thoughts that were once trapped by other's misunderstandings,

Now flow freely from your reserve,

New doors open with every detail written,

Empowering me through each deliberate word,

My voice that was once silenced, now screams bravely through you,

Confessing insecurities, desires, and fears,

Our bond has always been unbreakable, you are my deepest reflection,

And we will always remain as one until the ink runs dry.

VANITY

We live in a world of luxury, but we frown upon the vain,

We post images of our lives, without noticing we're the same,

We look at all of these celebrities and judge them by their wealth,

Yet, waste money on material things to feel better about ourselves,

We buy expensive clothes to cover up our pain,

And hide behind our makeup to mask us from the shame,

We brag about achievements and measure our success,

By how much's in our wallet and whose house looks the best,

We record our every move and the places that we've been,

And count our popularity by the number of our friends,

We workout in the gym and show off our nice physique,

And use a big vocabulary to impress them when we speak,

We dye our hair new colors to disguise all of the grey,

And try to preserve our youth in every possible way,

It's a shame we get caught up in all of this insanity,

And blind ourselves in a world full of all of our vanity!

WALDO

Sometimes I try to ignore the fact that I was affected by your absence,

How you chose to just disappear without a trace,

Me frantically searching for you throughout the years, but to no avail you were nowhere to be found,

I use to pretend that we were playing an extensive game of hide and seek and that one day I would find you,

How excited I would get if I thought I spotted you out in public,

That glimpse of hope evaporating as soon as I discovered it wasn't you,

I've lost that game to you many years ago because you are just that good at not being found,

I would've loved to call you daddy, father, or pops, but "Waldo" seems more fitting,

You can't imagine the pain I've endured over these years, "dad" I mean, "Waldo,"

Where are you?!

Every time we had a visitor at the door, I would race to open it hoping that you would be on the other side,

Anticipating the moment you would say to me, "I found you,"

Only to be greeted by the look of surprise on strangers' faces to discover that a child was so eager to see who it was,

Leaving me feeling embarrassed and angry because it was not you,

Sometimes I close my eyes and imagine how my life would've been with you in it,

If your presence would've affected me more than your absence,

Would I have been happier or more successful,

But, now I realize that it never was up to you to fulfill my purpose or to shape my destiny,

Because you've already done that by not showing up when I thought I needed you the most,

That hurt that I've been feeling for years was the fuel that I needed to strive harder in life,

The countless disappointments of your absence made me want to be present in everything I did,

The questions that I've always wanted to ask you, but I couldn't, made me go out and find my own answers,

The love that I thought I was missing made me love others so much more,

The words of encouragement that I didn't get encouraged me to speak affirmations in my life,

The warm hugs I never felt from you caused me to hug others a little tighter,

The kiss good night's I never received from you made me appreciate the kiss good morning's that much more,

All of these years, I felt weak not having you around,

But, now I realize you've made me stronger,

Your absence has been the biggest present in my life,

I no longer search for you in the crowd because for once, I've finally found me.

WATCHING OVER ME

Lord, I know you're with me even when I'm all alone,

You know my every thought even when they tend to roam,

You always watch over me even when my life's a mess,

You strengthen me through my trials and prepare me for hard tests,

I know I'm far from perfect, but you love me still the same,

And when I'm feeling troubled, I know to call upon your name,

You never leave me empty you fill me up with your pure love,

You send your spirit down to comfort me from the heavens up above,

I can always count on you to guide me through the righteous path,

You know my every need even before I have to ask,

You bless me every day even though I don't deserve it,

I praise your holy name because Lord you're truly worth it,

I should never feel afraid because you protect me day and night,

And when I'm blinded by the world you help me see your precious sight,

Thank you for my salvation and always thinking the best of me,

And sitting high while looking low as you watch over me.

WHAT IS EASTER TO ME

It's not about the Easter bunny or finding colorful eggs,

It's about the one who was mocked, beaten,

hung and bled,

No Easter bunny would sacrifice his life for you and I,

And then three days be resurrected from a tomb in which he lie,

It's not about chocolate candies and beautiful baskets filled with treats,

But about the one who gave his precious life for you and me,

It's more than just a day for us to wear our fancy clothes,

And style our children's hair real pretty with all of these colorful bows,

Is a day of remembrance for the one who gave so much,

To take our place upon that cross so that we would never touch,

It's the day that death was conquered by the only one who could,

A mission to us so impossible, but for him was understood,

Easter is not a holiday, but a day that needs correction,

For you see, my Savior lives, so I call it Happy Resurrection!

WHAT IS GRIEF

What is grief in the moment that you lose someone you love?

You weep all day and night and question God up above,

At first, you don't accept the fact they left you all alone,

Denying their very absence and that they are truly gone,

Anger becomes your friend and helps you build a wall of pain,

Keeping others out so you can find someone to blame,

Bargaining with God, you plead for Him to let them stay,

Your request remains ungranted, because life doesn't work this way,

Depression takes your hand and keeps you warm all through the night,

Withdrawing yourself from life, so that the darkness becomes your light,

Months and years go by, and you learn to live without their presence,

And finally, one day you come to a point of acceptance.

WHAT IT MEANS TO BE A VETERAN

What it means to be a Veteran is far beyond what meets the eye,

Soldiers giving up their lives to fight a war for you and I,

What it means to be a Veteran not too many will ever know,

The price they paid with their blood, a debt this country will

forever owe,

What it means to be a Veteran, an honorable act of sacrifice,

Trading their shoes for helmets and guns, freedom was the

highest price,

What it means to be a Veteran leaving their families all behind,

Fighting daily to keep our country free and safe for all of

mankind,

What it means to be a Veteran how they stared death in its face,

Losing companions during the fight, lives that cannot be replaced,

What it means to be a Veteran terrors of war keeping them awake,

Dodging bullets and enemy fire, praying death was not their fate,

What is means to be a Veteran how the war made some

depressed,

Some took their very own lives to finally have some peace and

rest,

What it means to be a Veteran some disabled and could not work,

Turning to prescription drugs to fill that void and ease the hurt,

What it means to be a Veteran bruises fade, but scars remain,

Fighting for red, white, and blue, liberty was the ultimate gain,

What it means to be a Veteran is more than just a holiday,

Because they chose to protect and serve we are all here today!

WHAT MY PASTOR MEANS TO ME

What my pastor means to me is more than what you know,

He's more than just a counselor who helps my spirit grow,

My pastor is a teacher of God's word with love and truth,

He's an example of Jesus Christ, the life he lives is proof,

The wisdom that he shares is evidence of God's pure love,

He leads his flock day and night with guidance from above,

My pastor is a vessel used to show the world God's light,

He never leads his flock astray or lets sin blind his sight,

My pastor is a caregiver, always tending to those in need,

He plants God's word in our hearts with the Holy Spirit's seed,

My pastor encourages others to always live right and do good,

And follow God's holy words, the way we really should,

My pastor is an example of what we all should strive to be,

And these few things are exactly what my pastor means to me.

WHEN YOU LOOK AT ME

When you look at me what do you see?

Is it my dark complexion that causes you to stare?

Or my full lips, broad nose, and coarse black hair,

Do you see me as failure when you look into my eyes?

Or another fatherless child whose hurt is disguised,

Do you see me as a threat, a thug, or a crook,

Or a high school drop out that can't read a book?

Do you see me as a statistic when you look into my face?

Or another lost cause that's just taking up space,

Do you see me as just another waste of your time?

Would you even talk to me or do you even mind?

You know what I see?

I see a young, black life that is destined to be great,

I see love in these eyes that have looked passed hate,

I see little, black children hoping for their family's freedom,

I see their parents crying out as their masters beat them,

I see slaves singing hymns longing for a new day,

I see wives on their knees teary-eyed as they pray,

I see Black, White, Brown and different shades of brothers,

I see the world coming together and getting along with one another,

I see the rise of Black leaders that helped pave our way,

From the Underground Railroad to our President today,

We were all created equal and that's how it should be,

I see no difference among us so why do you see one with me?

Alicia S. Azahar

WHERE DOES THE WIND COME FROM?

Many people ask this question because it's hard to understand,

Where does the wind come from that blows upon the land?,

This invisible force that's heard throughout the trees,

That gentle assurance of it's cool, cool breeze,

We can't see it, but we feel it on a dark stormy day,

Or during the spring as children run outside and play,

Where does the wind come from that blows upon the land?,

This incredible force not made by man,

It's mighty power is used for an assortment of things,

Energy, food, and other uses unseen,

Where does the wind come from that blows upon the land?,

A mystery to unfold in the eyes of man,

Hurricanes, tornadoes, and other natural disasters,

All use wind to make many things scatter,

Where does the wind come from that blows upon the land?,

This powerful force that can't be trapped by hands,

It blows from the north, south, east and west,

And gives speed to the sailboat out on a quest,

Where does the wind come from that blows upon the land?,

An answer to be given by the one who understands,

It gives power to the waves that crash upon the land,

And was told to be still by Jesus on command,

Where does the wind come from that blows upon the land?,

It was created by God's all powerful hands

WHO WOULD'VE KNOWN

There are love stories all around, but none were written of my own,

The thought of a "Happily Ever After" seemed so far away and gone,

But then you endowed me with your presence, who would've known you held the key,

A love story in the making, a lover disguised you would be,

Those seven words you dared to ask me, I never knew what was in store,

At that moment your presence was welcomed, led to another hidden door,

From our very first date, how confident you were at hand,

Unaware our stars aligned, you were destined to be my man,

We shared a connection far beyond, what false loves ever given me,

Who would've known, you'd be my "ever after" as our love story was written to be.

WINTER

Your heart reminds me of winter, the coldest season of the year,

Icicles of emotions form whenever I come near,

Your heart reminds of winter, so cold and very bleak,

Words destructive like an avalanche every time you speak,

Your heart reminds me of winter, black ice disguised by your smile,

A dangerous territory to uncover, like sharpened glass in a pile,

Your heart reminds me of winter, snowflakes fall but don't remain,

Empty streets of broken hearts, are paved by sleeting sheets of pain,

Your heart reminds me of winter, hailing sadness causing dents,

Shattered windows of broken promises, scattered by your ill-intent,

Your heart reminds me of winter, chilling down to the very bone

Leaving sickness in my body, the very moment you are gone.

WINTER STORM 2021

It came to our house like a thief in the night,

Turned off the heat and shut off the lights,

Such a chilling reality for one to discover,

As teeth clank and cold bodies shudder,

Howling winds pierce through its ice cold breath,

While piles of snow form incredible depths,

Black ice waits for its unaware prey,

As hands grip steering wheels and tires give way,

Frozen pipes hiss at the urge of a drip,

Clumsy feet stumble across ice and slip,

Icicles form like daggers on trees,

Footsteps are heard through the crunch of dead leaves,

Snowflakes fall like dust from a fan,

Whispering a thud as they carefully land,

Schools shut down forcing kids to stay home,

Parents call in to work as they groan,

A winter storm has come and it's here for a while,

Until it finds its next victim while out on a prowl

WOULD YOU TAKE JESUS WITH YOU?

If you went to a faraway country or to a place you didn't know,

Would you take Jesus with you everywhere that you would go?

Could you take Him to the liquor store or to the hottest club?

Or take Him to that street corner, or to the down-town pub,

Would you take Him to that party and let Him meet your friends?

Or would you fake an illness and pretend you couldn't attend?

Would you be ever so shameful of the things that you normally do?

And try to cover up the shame and things that were untrue,

Would you sneak Him in the backdoor and hope your friends didn't see,

The Holy, righteous person that you were trying to be?

Or would you leave Him at home and pretend you didn't know,

Would you take Jesus with you everywhere you go?

XANAX

I remember the first time I tried Xanax, a lady from work gave me half a pill,

At the time I was just a little anxious and she told me, "here this will help you chill,"

I didn't know much about it, I just wanted my anxiety to stop,

And not too long after I took it, it felt like everything just dropped,

Time just kind of slowed down for a moment, but then I felt very tired,

So then instead of me feeling anxious, I felt uninspired,

I thought "how can anyone function doped up on this medication?,"

Just to be a quarter productive would take a lot of concentration,

And to think that some people love to take it recreationally,

I hear rappers talk about it in their songs occasionally,

It literally took me a while to even come up with this poem,

So I can only imagine how long it takes for them to write a song,

What about the people who get prescribed to take it for a reason?,

Anxiety, depression, panic attacks and other disorders that need treating,

This is not just some drug to play with or to take at your disposal,

There are some people who can't function without it and would become antisocial,

Xanax is a sedative and can impact your coordination,

It can cause paranoia, memory impairment, and suicidal ideation,

Mix that with some alcohol and you might have a concoction for death,

And some people think it's fun to take without knowing the harm to self,

There are famous people who've passed away from mixing their medication,

With other drugs or alcohol, leaving the world in devastation,

Michael Jackson, Whitney Houston, Heath Ledger, and Kurt Cobain,

Erica Blasberg, Andy Irons, and others I haven't named,

Prescriptions are prescribed by doctors for a specific reason,

So don't take these drugs if you don't have a disorder that needs treating,

There are other drugs like Xanax that people take all around,

That have similar effects as it does most people have often found,

Some take Valium, Serax, Tranxene, and Lectopam,

Rivotril, Librium, Resoril, and Ativan,

This is just a list of different drugs used to treat anxiety,

The side effects may not be the same for you as it was for me,

Be aware of your health condition and don't take medicine from someone else,

But call your doctor to discuss a treatment that would be best for your health

YOU ARE WHAT YOU EAT

You are what you eat, but it's deeper than what you see,

The foods you put in your body hold an important key,

It's bigger than an occasional burger and your favorite chocolate shake,

You can still enjoy those foods, but balance is what it takes,

If you always eat fast foods you're doing an injustice to yourself,

Try a salad or some fruit to add more nutrients for your health,

If you're always feeling tired think about what meal you've had,

Saturated or salty foods can often make you feel real bad,

Ask your doctor for advice on which foods are good for you,

Use a food chart to help you out or you can seek a nutritionists too,

Some health issues come from poor eating habits so beware of what's on your plate,

Portion control is also important and can help to manage your weight,

High blood pressure, cholesterol, heart disease and a stroke,

All can come from eating bad so don't take your health as a joke,

Take control of your life so you can be healthy as can be,

And remember you can decide that you are what you eat!

YOU HAVE THE RIGHT TO REMAIN SILENT

You say I have the "right to remain silent," but I fear you mean forever,

I've heard too many stories where the evidence and report didn't go together,

You see, I left my house this morning and told my family "goodbye,"

I really meant to say, "see you later," not knowing today if I would die,

I was just minding my own business after a long day at work,

I didn't know you had a tough day and that's why you were being a jerk,

You pulled me over, but had no probable cause,

But because I "fit the description" my features gave you a pause,

You told me to get out of the car, but I didn't do nothing wrong,

And if I shut my mouth you would speed this process along,

I was so frustrated because I felt my rights were revoked,

So my hostility came at you whenever we spoke,

You took me as a threat even though I had no weapon,

But due to my appearance it gave you a negative perception,

I stared dead in your eyes and saw the fear on your face,

You don't know how bad it feels to be targeted because of your race,

Not all cops are bad, but they have a hell of a history,

Stories of traffic stops turning deadly is always a mystery,

Or standing up for ourselves because we feel mistreated,

Somehow leads to excessive force and us lying there bleeding,

What did we do so wrong that makes you feel so threatened?,

Does being black while driving count as having a weapon?,

We get plucked away from our families with one squeeze of the trigger,

And then the media paints us as bad in their black and white picture,

I refuse to live my life having to look over my shoulder,

But the way the system is set up our punishments seem to be colder,

A life sentence for a misunderstanding now what seems to be fair?,

Then you go on about your day like you don't even care,

What will it take for y'all to realize that our lives matter too?,

If you can't see the injustices then please walk a day in our shoes!

Alicia S. Azahar
YOUTH AGAINST VIOLENCE

We hear daily of the tragedies of our youth being slain,

How some turn to suicide to medicate their pain,

But are we taking a stand to intervene with this violence?

Or just turning our heads, choosing to be silent?

How often do we watch them being bullied in school?

The lack of discipline at home, the disregard for the rules,

Our police officers and teachers are made into villains,

Trading discipline and order for guns and killing,

The value of education is being reduced to a sentence,

Prison is the educator; there is no will for repentance,

Social media is being utilized to post videos of brutality,

People laughing and sharing as if it's a normality,

Are we not disgusted by such acts of violence?

No reprimands for abuse, just us choosing to stay silent,

How long will we sit on the sidelines of destruction?

Hoping violence decreases, but not aiding in its reduction,

Instead of condemning our youth for their disobedient ways,

Let's lead by example in what we do and not say!

We must take a stand and refuse to remain silent,

Let's join forces with our youth and stand against violence!

ABOUT THE AUTHOR

Alicia S. Azahar is a native of Louisiana, born on November 13, 1985, and raised in east Texas in a small town called Harleton. There she grew up with her five siblings Ashley, Patrick Jr, Aisha, Ashanti and Alijah. Prior to her growing up in east Texas, she resided in Hobbs, New Mexico, where her now deceased biological mother, Felicia Stoker, raised her and her older sister Ashley until her passing on April 26, 1994. Her biological mother, Felicia, was born in Terrell, TX and raised in Harleton, TX. She attended Wiley College in Marshall, TX, loved reading books and working out which definitely had a strong influence on Alicia. Her father, Patrick A. Johnson was born in Marshall, TX and raised in Harleton, TX and is the second youngest out of ten children. He served in the Air Force for almost ten years and works with youth through his non-profit organization called J S.T.A.R. Her mother, Shanna Johnson, was born and raised in Sulphur Springs, TX and is a basketball, cross country and track coach at Harleton High School. Alicia participated in sports all throughout her school career and excelled in UIL competitions including Poetry Interpretation, Public Speaking and the One Act Play. She has a strong background in the church as her father is a minister. Alicia sung in the church choir, praised danced and attended church functions all throughout her childhood. She developed a skill for writing when her mother passed away and she was taken to get help to cope with her grief. It was through pen and paper that her healing began and she has not put it down since. Alicia went on to attend Kilgore College and Tyler Junior College where she received her associate degree. She became pregnant while in college and gave birth to her daughter Katrice. A few years later she went on to give birth to a second child, her son, Kai. Alicia was in a domestic violence relationship but has since left with her children and is now married to her husband Gilbert Azahar. They met while working at Capital One call center in Irving, TX. Writing has always been her first love and she decided to create her own business through the vision God gave her. From that was born Uninterrupted Thoughts that helps people express themselves through journaling and the art of Spoken word. In her spare time, Alicia teaches a Social and Emotional Intervention class at the local high school, participates in Open mic nights, guest speaks at events, schools and has also won second place in a Poetry Slam at Black and Bitter Coffee in Duncanville, TX. Alicia's goal is to touch as many lives as she can through her gifts of writing and poetry by "making an impression one thought at a time."